Drogheda
Gateway to the Boyne

Paintings by Paul McCann & Stories by Seán Collins

Cottage Publications

First published by Cottage Publications,
Donaghadee, N. Ireland 1998.
Copyrights Reserved.
© Illustrations by Paul McCann 1998.
© Text by Seán Collins 1998.
Design & origination in Ireland.
Printed & bound in Singapore.

ISBN 1 900935 08 2

The Author

Seán Collins is a graduate of University College Dublin and is currently studying for a post-graduate degree there. His specialisation is Revolutionary Ireland.

Since 1989 he is Chairman of the Old Drogheda Society and a director of Millmount Museum Limited. He organises the John Boyle O'Reilly Summer School every June and the ODS Historical Symposium in September. He has published in the past in the Journal of the Old Drogheda Society and the Drogheda Independent.

Seán and his wife Linda, with their three children Seán Óg, Dearbhla and Pádraig, live in Drogheda.

The Artist

Paul McCann graduated in 1992 from the College of Marketing & Design with a Diploma in Fine Art, specialising in painting.

Since then he has taken part in various exhibitions around the country. He also spent a year painting and living in South America. His work is normally of a modern nature, but commissioned pieces cover all styles and disciplines. Teaching and working with the Drogheda Arts Centre keeps him busy.

Paul and his wife Sharon live in Drogheda.

Contents

Legends of Drogheda & The Boyne Valley   **3**

Paintings and Stories from the Land of Boann

Site of the Battle of the Boyne	12	Saint Peter's Church of Ireland	42
Dowth	14	The Court-house, Fair Street	44
Newgrange	16	The Viaduct	46
Knowth	18	Millmount Museum	48
Slane	20	Saint Mary's, James' Street	50
Collon	22	Clarkes, Peter Street	52
Melifont	24	Mayoralty House (Sound Shop)	54
Monasterboice	26	The Barlow House	56
Clogherhead	28	The Thatch	58
Termonfeckin	30	Ballsgrove Gate	60
Laurence's Gate	32	Mornington	62
Magdalene Tower	34	Laytown	64
The Old Abbey	36	Julianstown	66
West Street and St. Peter's	38	Duleek	68
The Tholsel	40	Donore	70

The People of Drogheda   **73**

Sources   **90**

Legends of Drogheda & The Boyne Valley

Drogheda, an Anglo-Norman town, developed in the 1180s and formally chartered by Walter de Lacy in 1194, is a relatively modern town when compared to the ancient valley of the Boyne to which it has become the gateway. For long before the early Christian monks began to write down the history of Ireland, the Boyne was noted in the long oral tradition of myth and legend. Our earliest legends are those categorised as the mythological cycle, the stories of the Tuatha de Danann. These stories are full of tragedy and romance, they tell of a world full of magic and evil. One story tells of how the River Boyne was formed.

In the centre of a large forest in Kildare lay an ancient well said to have been blessed by the Tuatha de Danann. The well was more ancient then the forest itself and five hundred staunch oak trees surrounded and protected it. Its waters were magical with curative powers that were legendary. Many kings and chieftains had endeavoured to take control of the well, so the druids determined that only one clan should care for the well and preserve its magical powers. It was also decreed that the well's waters should only be used in time of plague because misuse of this precious liquid had caused its level to drop dangerously low. A crystal wall was built around the well and a beautiful wooden cover worked with gold was placed on top to stop any of the precious waters escaping. The Clan Nectain were the curators of the well and as it hadn't been used for many centuries they were the only ones that knew of its whereabouts. Nectain, the eldest of the four remaining brothers of the clan, was an old and experienced warrior who had spent a lifetime protecting and guarding the well.

As was the tradition of the time, a marriage was arranged and Nectain married Boann, a beautiful young woman of sixteen years, who Nectain had little regard for, as he had been forced to marry her. They had been married barely a month when Boann, being an inquisitve young woman, queried the whereabouts of the secret well. That day Nectain had bathed in the stream that ran close to their house. He dressed himself in new clothes and removed all metals from his garments. Boann, from her studies of magical lore, knew that metals could not be brought near places of magic power, and that the warrior and his clothing had to be spotlessly clean.

"I'll be back at dawn", Nectain said as he was leaving the house. *"Where are you going"*, Boann asked. *"I am going to the ancient well in the forest, to perform the duties of the caretaker of the well, as has been performed by the Clan Nectain for many centuries"*. *"Take me with you"*, she said. Nectain shook his head saying, *"I cannot, you know it is forbidden for any other but a member of the Clan Nectain to approach the magical well"*. *"But I am your wife"*, she said, *"I am now part of the clan"*. Nectain replied. *"Our children, should we have children, will be able to go to the well because they are of my blood, but you are not"*.

In the months that followed, Boann carefully observed the comings and goings of her husband, for she was determined to find her way to the magical well. Her attitude towards her husband seemed to change, and she became a more obedient, loving wife however, Nectain did not realise this was part of her plan to gain access to the well.

One dark night, Boann followed the Clan Nectain closely as they went to visit the well. When they reached their destination she hid patiently in the bushes until Nectain and his brothers carried out their ancient rituals. When they finished, and had departed the scene, Boann slowly approached the well. It was surrounded by a circle of standing stones, but the crystal wall was streaked with dirt and the gold on the lid was dull and peeling. Boann was dissappointed, she believed all the magic from the well was gone. She pushed back the lid and gazed into the well. She drank water from the well and broke the ancient law, that deemed only the Clan Nectain could drink the water, and immediately the stone circle came to life. The stones became monsters and surrounded Boann

and she stood in horror at the sight. The monsters began to crowd in on her, but there was nowhere to run. Boann was pushed up against the wall of the well. She tumbled backwards and fell into it. Suddenly there was silence, and then the earth began to tremble like an earthquake. The well erupted like a volcano, casting its waters high into the air. People who lived in the area who had been drawn to the spectacle by the noise, said that the column of water that rose from the well resembled a young, wild haired woman. Only Nectain recognised his wife in the deluge. The water surged through the county of Meath, sweeping all before it, swallowing whole communities of people and cattle alike, until it burst into the sea.

No one knew where the river had come from, but magic forces still dominated the landscapes of Ancient Ireland, and ordinary men could only accept these acts of the gods, and hence the river Boyne was formed.

Perhaps the most popular legends of Irish folklore are the tales of the boy warrior Cu-Cuchaillin, categorised as the 'Ulster' or 'Warrior Cycle'. Again the mystical River Boyne is featured. In the first legend of this cycle, we learn of the conception and birth of Cu-Cuchaillin on the banks of the river. Conchobar, the king of Ulster, was at his capital Emain Macha preparing for the marriage of his sister, Dechtire, to Sualtam, the brother of Fergus McRoth. It was late in the evening, and Dechtire was thirsty. She decided to drink some wine, and as she was drinking it, a mayfly flew into the cup, which she swallowed along with the wine. Afterwards, she went to her parlour, with her fifty maidens, and fell into a deep sleep. In this sleep, she was visited by Lugh, the god of light, from whom the County of Louth got its name. Lugh

told her, *"I was the mayfly that flew into your drink, now you and your maidens must follow me"*. He transformed them into a flock of birds and they went with him to Brugh na Boinne, the magical burial ground on the banks of the River Boyne. Here they stayed and no one at Emain Macha, knew what had become of them.

One year passed, and Conchobar gathered all his nobles at Emain Macha for a feast. As they enjoyed the feast they spied through the window a great flock of birds descending on the plain and eating all their crops, they left not as much as a blade of grass standing. The men of Ulster rose in anger, they prepared their chariots and with Conchobar at the lead they began to chase the flock of mischievous birds. They travelled south and as they did they noticed there were nine flocks of birds in all. Each was linked by silver chains and at the head of each flock were two birds of different colours linked by a gold chain. In front of all these were three birds that flew alone leading the entire formation towards Brugh na Boinne. It grew dark and the birds vanished from the sky. Conchobar ordered his men to dismount. He sent Bricriu, one of his warriors, to seek shelter. Bricriu found a small house where an old couple requested him to bring his companions and share their hospitality. He advised Conchobar there was little point in accepting this offer unless they could bring their own provisions.

When Conchobar and the men of Ulster went to the house they found a large building and were greeted by a fine young man in a suit of armour, completely different to what Bricriu had described. There was plenty of food and they were well entertained. Conchobar enquired after the mistress of the house. The young man explained that he could not see her because she was in the pangs of childbirth. Later in the night could be heard throughout the house the cry of a new born infant. At the same time a mare gave birth to two foals. The men of Ulster decided to keep the foals and present them as a gift to the child. The next morning Conchobar was the first to rise and he went in search of his host but could not find him. Hearing the baby cry in a side room he went in to see it. There, to his amazement he found Dechtire with her maidens and the new baby. She explained to him how they had been spirited away from Emain Macha by Lugh and he had been the young man that had greeted Conchobar the evening before.

Conchobar decided that they should all return to Emain Macha to consult Morann, the judge, on the issue of who should care for the child. Morann's judgement was trusted and believed, for round his neck he wore a torc that would tighten if he gave a false judgement. Morann decreed that Conchobar should raise the child for being Dechtire's brother, he was next of kin. He said the child would be praised by all and that he would defend Ulster. The name he was given was Cú Chulainn, and he was raised on the plain of Muirthemne having been born on the banks of the Boyne.

The legend most synonymous with the River Boyne is 'Fionn McCumaill and the Salmon of Knowledge'. These legends, known as the 'Fionn Cycle', are very similar to the Arthurian legends in England. They tell of the warrior King Fionn, his Red Branch Knights and their daring exploits. Fionn is the one character in all of Irish folklore who seems to overcome legend, as he emerges in tales of Cormac Mac Art, a genuine third century king of Tara.

In ancient Ireland young men trained to be warriors and hunters but it was also deemed fitting that they should learn the art of poetry and for this reason, the young warrior Fionn MacCumhaill travelled to the house of Finnegas, an old druid who lived by the banks of the Boyne. Finnegas had lived there for many years trying to catch the Salmon of Knowledge, for it had been prophesied that whoever ate the salmon in its entirety, would be blessed with boundless knowledge and wisdom. The prophecy also said that the salmon would be eaten by someone named Finn, and Finnegas naturally assumed this referred to him. He did not worry therefore when a young man named Demna, (the birth name of Fionn McCumhaill), requested to be his pupil. He took the boy into his home and started to teach him all he knew about the art of poetry and rhyme making.

The wonderful day arrived at last when

Finnegas landed the Salmon of Knowledge. It was a much larger fish than he had ever seen before and on its shiny skin, could be seen all the colours of the rainbow. Finnegas carried the fish back to his house and ordered his young pupil to cook it. He was careful to advise the young man that the fish was for himself alone and that on no account was Fionn to taste it. Demna did as he was instructed and in a short time the smell of cooking salmon wafted through the house. As the fish was cooking a large blister bubbled up on its side. Demna burst the blister with his thumb and in doing so he burnt his thumb, immediately putting his thumb in his mouth and sucked it to ease the burning pain. When Fionn brought the Salmon before Finnegas he was asked if he had sampled it. He explained about the blister and how he had sucked his thumb but he said that he hadn't eaten any of it. Finnegas advised him that as he had tasted the salmon first, he would gain all the knowledge and so he should eat it all. Finnegas however could not understand how a Demna had come to eat the fish and not a Fionn, as the prophecy said. Demna explained that Fionn meaning 'the fair one', was his nickname as he had fair hair, and so the prophecy was fulfilled.

The final saga of the Boyne that best describes the transition from the mystical Ireland of Finn and Cú-Chulainn, is the story of King Cormac and his desire to be buried at Rossnaree, and not at Brugh na Boinne, the traditional burial ground of kings. Sir Samuel Ferguson, in his poem 'The Burial of King Cormac', best expressed the King's desire;

"Spread not the beds of Brugh for me,
When restless deathbeds use is done,
But bury me at Rossnaree,
And face me to the Rising Sun".

However the King's advisors did not take much note of this and poetry tells us;

"Dear Cormac on his bier they laid,
He reigned a king for forty years,
And shame it were, hi captain said
He lay not with his royal peers
His grandsire, Hundred – Battle, sleeps
Serene in Brugh; and, all around,
Dead kings in stone sepulchral keeps,
Protect the sacred burial keeps,

What though a dying man should rave,
Of changes ore the Eastern Sea,
In Brugh of Boyne shall be his grave,
And not in noteless Rossnaree"

Four times they tried to bring the King's coffin across the river, and four times the river seemed to defy them;

"While as a youth with practice spear,
Through jostling crowds bears oft the ring,

Boyne from their shoulders caught the bier,
And proudly bore away the king.

At morning, on the grassy marge,
Of Rossnaree the corpse was found,
And shepherds at their early charge,
Entombed it in the peaceful ground.

Round Cormac, spring renews her buds;
In March perpetual by her side,
Down come the earth fresh April floods,
And up the sea fresh salmon glide."

So Cormac's wish was fulfilled and he was buried facing the rising sun, the direction in which the saviour would appear on the last day.

In 432 it is said that Saint Patrick came to Ireland at the instructions of the Pope to preach Christianity to the natives, and minister to those already converted. Recent revision now suggests that Patrick possibly came on a later date, nearer to 470 in fact. However, the stories remain the same. It is believed he arrived in Ireland by way of the River Boyne and settled for his first night in Ireland on the Hill of Slane, overlooking the river. It was the time of the pascal feast and the countryside waited for the King on the hill of Tara to light the Pascal Fire, and then all other fires could be lighted. Saint Patrick, not being aware of this, lit a fire on the Hill of Slane. The King on nearby Tara, sent his warriors to capture the person who had broken the ancient law. They captured Patrick and brought him to Tara. Patrick explained to the old King the coming of the new faith and indeed here at Tara he first used the shamrock to explain the Holy Trinity, forever to remain his emblem. Later, Patrick would meet Oisín returning from the land of Tír na nÓg when he heard Saint Patrick's bell ring to signal the coming of Christianity; and the end of the land of mysticism and magic.

The site of the Battle of the Boyne, 1690, was once dominated by a very fine obelisk. Standing 110 feet high, and commemorating the victory of William III at this site in July of 1690, the inscription read;

"Sacred to the Glorious Memory
of
King William III.

Who on the 1st of July 1690 crossed the Boyne near this place to attack James II at the head of a popish army, and advantageously posted at the south side of it, and did on that day, by a successful battle, secure to us and our posterity our liberty, laws and religion. In consequence of this action, James II left this kingdom and fled to France. This memorial of our deliverance was erected in the ninth year of the reign of King George II, the first stone being laid by Lionel Sackville, Duke of Dorset, Lord Lieutenant of the Kingdom of Ireland."

The author of the above text provided a somewhat simplistic view of the issues relevant to the Battle of the Boyne. This battle, effectively a skirmish by battle standards of it's time did indeed see William defeat James. However, it should be noted that the battle was part of a struggle for kingship. James II, the legitimate King of England and Ireland had been usurped by his son-in-law William of Orange.

Here at the Boyne was fought the most famous battle of the period known as the 'Williamite Wars', to secure the kingship for one side or the other. In the aftermath of this battle James II fled to France, effectively removing the threat to William's kingship and giving the battle its significance. On the day, combined losses of both armies was just under 1,100 men. Barely one year later at Aughrim, 11,000 were killed and yet the Boyne is the more noted battle.

The Obelisk was blown up in June 1923 and at the time this event was blamed on the I.R.A.. However in the mid 1970s, a group of retired regular army officers, acknowledged their involvement.

Site of the Battle of the Boyne

In 1844 at Dowth, to William David O'Reilly and his wife Elizabeth was born a son, John, he was their second, in a family of three boys and five girls. William worked as a teacher in a school for orphans in the Netterville Institute. All the young O'Reillys grew up and were educated in the institute.

When he was 11 years old, John was an apprentice compositor on the Drogheda Argus newspaper. To complete his apprenticeship he went to Preston, England, where he stayed with his aunt, and worked at the Preston Guardian. He later joined the British army and his regiment was posted to Dundalk, Co. Louth. When back in Ireland, he joined the Fenian movement and became active in recruiting among his army comrades for that organisation. Having been unmasked as a spy, he was sentenced to death, but this was commuted to life imprisonment because of his young age, being barely twenty. He was transported to Western Australia aboard the 'Hougomont', the last ship to bring Fenian prisoners to the south seas.

He was placed in Bunbury camp, and soon was employed as a librarian. It was here in Australia that he started to write poetry and some prose.

Always anxious to get back to Ireland, O'Reilly managed to escape from Australia, on board an American whaling ship. He arrived in America, penniless, but free, and with the help of Clan na Gael he soon got a job at the 'Boston Pilot'. He worked first as a reporter, then as editor and eventually came to have a half share in the newspaper. He helped make the Pilot, an important and influential newspaper, not only among Irish-Americans, but also espousing the causes of Red Indians, Jews, and oppressed people everywhere.

He never returned to Ireland, but he never forgot his home at Dowth, one of the most beautiful places on the Boyne.

Dowth

The late Professor Frank Mitchell once estimated that 15,000 able-bodied men lifting 750 sacks of stone or earth, working twelve hours a day, and six days a week, could build the great mound at Newgrange in five to six years, depending on how far they had to transport the material. More recent research has shown that the white stones surrounding the mound were gathered in Wicklow and brought to Newgrange along the coast and up the River Boyne on rafts. This information would surely indicate the need for further adjustment of Prof. Mitchell's calculations.

The burial mound at Newgrange was once surrounded by a ring of standing stones, estimated at 38, although only 12 remain, all standing eight feet in height. The mound covers one acre of ground, is 280ft in diameter and upwards on 40ft in height. Radio-carbon dating indicates the mound was built about 3000 BC, making it about four hundred years older than the pyramids and subsequently the oldest man-made building in the world. The passage to the central chamber is 62 feet long and three side chambers opening from it are walled with big stone slabs, many of which are decorated.

In early excavations at the entrance to Newgrange a variety of Roman gold coins and ornaments were found. Some suggest these were votive offerings left by Irishmen returning from raids on Britain. Traditionally we have been told, by Gibbon onwards, that the Romans never came to Ireland. The Greco-Egyptian map-maker Ptolemy, in his map of Ireland, included Buvinda, easily identifiable as the Boyne. He explained that while he had never been to Ireland, Venetian traders gave him the details for his map in the 1st Century AD. If Venetian traders made it to the Boyne, then surely Romans did as well and left their coins and ornaments as tributes to the gods of Brugh na Boinne.

Newgrange

Along with Dowth and Newgrange, Knowth makes up the three great burial sites in the pre-historic cemetery of Brugh na Boinne. The site at Knowth is different from the other two in the sense that it went through three periods of important settlement, and excavations at the site produced evidence of all three. Firstly, it had its beginnings in the Neolithic period, and the tomb and passage graves remain as evidence of this age. Secondly, it was populated from the Iron-Age right through to the early Christian period, and up to the coming of the Anglo-Normans. It was the headquarters of the Kings of Northern Bregia, and for this reason it is believed that the Vikings did not settle on the Boyne, instead moving further south, to the river Liffey, away from the threat of the hordes of Bregia.

The third period of settlement at Knowth, started with the arrival of the Anglo-Normans in the late 1100s, who built a castle on top of the main mound. Surviving remains show that the walls were five to six feet thick, and the building was 120 feet in circumference externally. Upwards on 70% of all the meglithic rock art to be found in Europe is here at Knowth, but the meaning of the drawings and inscriptions have puzzled scholars for years.

Professor George Eogan has led the excavations at Knowth since 1962. Long may his valuable work continue.

When young Mr Caddell of Harbourstown came of age, it was felt appropriate that a young man of his quality should take the "grand tour", and visit the continent. In 1795, Michael O'Hanlon, a native of Dowth, having graduated at Bordeaux was appointed curate of Slane. The Bishop granted Fr. O'Hanlon leave of absence to accompany Mr Caddell on his continental travels.

Dean Cogan in his extensive writings noted that O'Hanlon and Caddell stayed at the Irish college in Paris, Fr. O'Hanlon being a friend of the college President. While enjoying an evening repast they heard a voice enquiring did anybody know a Colonel Conyngham from Ireland. Fr. O'Hanlon said that he did, and he was brought to a military tribunal. Addressing the tribunal, O'Hanlon gave Conyngham and his family much credit for their liberality and kindness to their tenants. On account of this, Colonel Conyngham was set free. When the 'grand tour' ended, Fr. O' Hanlon returned to Slane as parish priest.

In 1798, Cogan records *the mass house fell suddenly in the beginning of the year, and the inhabitants were for a considerable time without any place of worship"*. Colonel Conyngham now succeeded to his inheritance of the Slane estate, and when he was visited by Fr. O'Hanlon, he acknowledged that the priest had saved his life. He asked Fr. O'Hanlon, if there was any favour he required, where upon O'Hanlon explained his people had only a barn to worship in and he needed a church. Conyngham gave him a site and helped build a church. A newspaper notice of 1802 records;

> *"On the 8th inst at Slane, the foundation stone of a Roman Catholic Chapel was laid by Lord Mount Charles, son to the Earl of Conyngham, on a plot of ground which the Earl had generously granted for that purpose. To witness the ceremony, a vast concourse of spectators were assembled, who testified their gratitude and affection to his Lordship, by repeated cheers. The chapel is to be called Mount Charles in a compliment to the young nobleman who laid the foundation stone".*

Lord Mount Charles was 7 years of age at this time.

Slane

The village of Collon was originally part of the Lordship of Mellifont. In 1172, Henry II granted lands here to the Cistercians of Mellifont and, in 1203, King John gave a charter allowing a weekly market to be held here.

On the 23rd of July 1539, the Cistercian Abbey at Mellifont, under the dissolution, with all its lands was given to Lord Viscount Drogheda. The village of Collon was eventually sold by the Moores to the Foster family who established Collon as their family seat.

John Foster was elected MP for Louth in 1768, and went on to be the last speaker of the Irish House of Commons prior to the Act of Union, 1801. Foster was an astute businessman and he brought much prosperity to Collon. He started a bleaching green here in 1780, and developed a number of textile mills in and around the area. The steady employment and prosperity of Collon at this time encouraged great growth in the population and the further development of the area.

In 1938, the Cistercian Order of Mount Mellary Oriel Temple, purchased the once proud home of the Speaker Foster. A group of monks under Father Benignus Hickey arrived here on the 4th November of that year, and set about re-establishing the order in the area. It was exactly 300 years since their fellow Cistercians had been forced to leave the area by the dissolution. Also in 1938 Collon provided the first home of the Medical Missionaries of Mary, who later established their headquarters in Drogheda.

In light of this year being the bicentenary of the 1798 Rebellion, it is interesting to note that the leader of the United Irishmen in the area, Michael Boylan, a native of Blackestown, Ardee, was captured in Collon. A ballad in his memory recalls;

"In Collon I was taken, it was on the
4th of June
The Drogheda Guards that brought me
Back, 'till I received my doom
I'd been in expectation, Speaker Foster
would set me free,
'Till I received my sentence through Dan
Kelly's perjury."

Collon

In the Spring of 1140, Malachy O'Morgair, Bishop of Down and one time Archbishop of Armagh set out with a number of disciples to visit the Pope in Rome.

On his journey he went to Clairvaux in France to visit St. Bernard. Malachy was so impressed by the lifestyle of the monks, he desired to resign his position and become a simple monk. However, the Pope would not accept this, and ordered Malachy to return to Ireland and continue his work there.

On his journey home Malachy once again visited Clairvaux. This time be left four of his brethren with Bernard, requesting that they be trained in the Cistercian life Malachy was anxious to see the Cistercians established in Ireland as soon as possible, and in correspondence, Bernard requested him to seek out a suitable site for a monastery, *"Far removed from the turmoil of the world"*.

Malachy chose a sight on the banks of the Mattock River, a tributary of the Boyne, and here in this secluded spot known as Melifont, the first Cistercian Abbey in Ireland was built and established in 1142. The first Abbot was Giolla Criost O' Conairche, and the abbey became so well established that by 1152, the synod of Drogheda was held here.

In 1157 a gathering of the kings of Ireland took place in Mellifont for the consecration of the Abbey Church, by Gillamacliag Mac Ruaidhri, the Archbishop of Armagh. According to the annals of the Four Masters,

"there were present seventeen bishops, together with the legate and successor of Patrick and the number of persons of every other decree was countless."

The abbey was closed in 1539 under the Henrican dissolution, although records show the Cistercians lived secretly in and around the Drogheda area right up to 1641.

Famous for its high crosses and round tower, Monasterboice was established sometime in the latter half of the 5th century. The name Monasterboice is a corruption of the Latin Monasteruim Boecii (the monastery of Boecius). The Saint, Boecius, is in the Irish form styled Buithe.

It is not known when exactly the monastery was founded, but it is known that Buithe died on the 7th December, 521 AD, the day Colum Cille was born. So it is generally accepted that Monasterboice was founded by Buithe in the late 400s. Buithe was born on the banks of the Boyne, in the townland of Mell, Drogheda. The annals tell us, his father wanted the child to be baptised. He spotted two holy men approaching by boat, and he called them, requesting that they baptise the child. They pointed out that they could not baptise him in the river, because the water was salty, the Boyne being tidal as far inland as Townley Hall and fresh water was required for baptism. Then one of the holy men took the child and stuck his finger into the ground, a freshwater spring arose from the hole, and so Buithe was baptised a Christian. The townland of Mell today has a laneway leading to a well, used by the townspeople for many centuries, known as Tubberboice Lane, an Anglicisation of Tobair Buithe, the Well of Boice.

The graveyard at Monasterboice has been in use since its foundation, making it possibly the oldest graveyard in constant use in Ireland. In the grounds can be found two of the finest high crosses in Ireland dated to the 10th century. The round tower has five storeys, and the two ruined old churches in the grounds date to the 10th and 13th centuries respectively.

Monasterboice

"Is Clogherhead like it used to be
Is the pier still there,
Do the boys and girls go 'round the
head in the evening fair,
Is my girl as nice as she used to be,
Are my friends all right,
O! what I'd give to be with them
in Clogherhead tonight."

The emigrant's longing for home recalled in this simple ballad about Clogherhead, a coastal fishing village in south Co. Louth. In the early 1880s, Lord Masserene requested the government of the day to provide funding to build a proper pier at Clogherhead. The work was completed in 1885 at the cost of £17,000. It was announced recently that £1,000,000 is to be spent to renew the harbour, no one could deny that £17,000 has given 110 years of value.

Clogherhead is noted in South Louth as the base for the lifeboat. The lifeboat station was opened there in 1889, and the first lifeboat was called the 'Charles Whitton'. Since its inception, over twelve lifeboats have patrolled the coasts of Co. Louth from their base in Clogherhead, answering distress calls in all types of weather.

The current lifeboat at Clogherhead is called the 'Doris Bleasdale' and it arrived there on Friday 12th February 1993. It will carry the lifeboat service at Clogherhead into the new millennium and past 1999, a hundred years since the arrival of the 'Charles Whitton'.

In the cemetery of Mayne near Clogherhead this most amusing epitaph recalls the life of one interred there;

"Beneath this stone there lieth one, That still his friends did please
To heaven I hope his soul is gone, To enjoy eternal ease
He drank, he sang while here on earth, lived happy as a lord,
And now he hath resigned his breath, God rest you Paddy Ward".

The tombstone is dated 1793.

Clogherhead

Termonfeckin with it's much maligned title is without doubt one of the most picturesque villages of Co. Louth. It gets it's name from St. Fechin, who, it is said founded a monastery here in the 7th century AD. The name Termonfeckin is an anglicisation of the Irish Tearmann Feichin, which would translate as 'the sanctuary of Fechin'.

It is noted in the *"Annals of the Four Masters,"* that the monastery in Termonfeckin was attacked by Vikings in 1013 and 1025. In 1149 it was attacked by the men of Bregia. However, in 1164, the King of Oriel, Donnabhadh O'Carroll placed 'canons regular' in it, confirming its dedication to St. Fechin.

Edward I decreed that henceforth no Irishman could be appointed archbishop of Armagh, because; *"He doth preach against the king"*

Subsequently Normans were appointed to fulfill the role. The new Archbishops however were not welcome in Armagh, indeed the Dean and Chapter at Armagh would not let them in and so they moved south to Termonfeckin. A palace was erected on the banks of the river, which remained in use until 1656. During the Catholic Rebellion in the 1640s, upwards of 100 people were killed in the village. The nearby town of Drogheda was besieged by the Confederates in 1641, and a great deal of skirmishing took place, perhaps it was on one of these skirmishes the villagers were killed.

In modern times Termonfeckin is traditionally identified as the home of the Irish Countrywomen's Association. Its headquarters at An Grianan, is a hive of activity throughout the year. The house, originally known as Newtown House, was once the home of the Smyths and the McClintocks. It even served as a hotel, until the Kellogg Foundation purchased it for the I.C.A.

Termonfeckin

The great east gate of Drogheda stands majestically at the top of Great East Street. Now, both street and gate are known as St. Laurence's after the medieval friary of St. Laurence's that existed on the Cord Road in the early 14th century. A drawing by Francis Place of Drogheda in 1699, shows the West Gate to be almost identical to St. Laurence's Gate. This gate or barbican as it exists today has been described as the finest piece of medieval architecture in these islands.

The gate dated 1250 is based on the murage grants issued to the town from 1234 onwards. The murage grant allowed the corporation to levy a tax on incoming goods to help pay for the building of town defences. On the south side of the street, in line with what would have seen the inner gate of the barbican, is a fine example of town wall complete with buttress. This part of town wall now leading into a cul de sac, marks the line of the lane that led to the well of St. Elena mentioned in the Gomanston Register.

The hospital priory of St. Laurence the Martyr was founded in Drogheda in 1202 by the monks of the order, Fratres Cruciferi, an order of hospitallers with congregations throughout England and Ireland. In 1300, Martin de Termonfeckin killed Laurence de Hell in the dwelling house of the master of this priory, and he immediately took sanctuary in the church of St. Mary's Hospital. While there is no further information on what happened to Martin, we can only assume things weren't always peaceful in the priory. On the dissolution, John Goldsmith, presumably the last prior, was granted a pension of four pounds per annum. Laurence's Hospital was originally for lepers who were transferred there from the hospital of St. Mary Magdalene at Sunday's Gate.

Laurence's Gate

The Dominican Friars came to Ireland in 1224 and established houses at Drogheda and Dublin. They expanded rapidly throughout the country and, by the year 1300, had 24 houses throughout Ireland.

In Drogheda the Priory of St. Mary Magdalene was founded by Luke Netterville, the Archbishop of Armagh, and its great steeple has dominated the northern skyline of Drogheda since. In 1394, four Irish chieftains made their submission to Richard II in this Friary. A description of the scene tells of the King, with his forked planta-genet beard and flowing robes, accepting the sub-mission of the gaelic chieftains in their saffron cloaks, casting their scians, or short swords, at his feet.

The establishment of the town of Drogheda in 1194 by Walter de Lacy, saw effectively the devel-opment of two towns, one each side of the river. Drogheda in Meath and Drogheda in Oriel. So they developed, one ruled by a mayor, the other by a senschal with consistant competition between both. In 1412, a Dominican, named Philip Bennet, a master of theology, invited the townspeople to come together and live in peace and harmony. This proposal was accepted by all, and in that year a unification charter was issued by the King and the two towns became one. In 1468 a parliament held in Drogheda passed an act granting an annual sum to the friary as it had fallen into decay and poverty, through incessant depredations of English enemies and Irish rebels.

After the suppression, there is evidence to show that the Dominicans maintained a presence in Drogheda right up to 1640 and appeared again in 1670.

Magdalene Tower

The hospital and priory of St. Mary d'Urso was founded in Drogheda in 1206. Ursus de Swemele, a wealthy resident of the town funded and founded the establishment. Today it is commonly referred to as the 'Old Abbey'.

In the medieval period, five hospitals were established in Drogheda. One at the Magdalene Friary on the north side, St. James's and St. John's on the south side, St. Laurence's to the east, and the hospital here at St. Mary d'Urso. With the building of town walls after the murage grant of 1234, some of the hospital/friaries, were incorporated inside the town walls, notably St. James's, St. Mary Magdalene's, and St. Mary d'Urso.

The last prior of the abbey was one Nicholas Corbaly, who at the dissolution was granted a pension of £5 pounds per annum. There are no further records to show what may have happened to the inmates of the hospital, if indeed there were any.

Extensive excavations were carried out at the site in 1989 and for the first time a collection of skeletal material from the town, could be examined. The remains of both males and females were found on the site, and the Irish Times carried the story that the remains of victims of the Cromwellian Slaughter in 1649 had been found.

In 1556 the priory buildings was granted to the mayor and corporations of Drogheda along with the hospital of St. Laurence and the Carmelite friary.

The Old Abbey

In 1645, Oliver Plunkett, a native of Loughcrew, County Meath, was sent to Rome to pursue his religious studies. He was accepted as a student in the Irish College where he studied mathematics, philosophy and theology. He was ordained in 1654, and in 1657 he was appointed professor in the college of the Propaganda Fide, where he lectured for twelve years. At forty years of age he was appointed Archbishop of Armagh and in mid-March, 1670, he returned to Ireland twenty-five years after his departure. He established a Jesuit college at Drogheda and became active in reorganising the church.

An act of parliament in 1673, decreed that all popish bishops and clergy should depart from the kingdom. Plunkett persevered, however, he wrote;

"I am morally certain that I should be taken; so many are in search of me yet in spite of danger I will remain with my flock"

He was eventually captured in Dublin and having been brought to England, was tried and found guilty of high treason. He was taken to Tyburn and hung, drawn and quartered.

Doctor Plunkett was beatified on the 23rd of May, 1920, and proclaimed a saint on the 12th of October, 1973. The very fine parish church of St. Peter, in West Street, is also known as the St. Oliver Plunkett Memorial Church. The foundation stone of the church was laid on the 10th of July, 1881, to commemorate the bicentenary of the martyrdom of Doctor Oliver Plunkett. The head of the martyred primate and other relics are kept in the church.

West Street and St. Peter's

"There's a place down in Drogheda, and the Tholsel it's called,
Where the boys all stand there, with their backs to the wall,
They come down from the labour, and they gather to talk,
But you won't get no news, standing under the clock"

Local balladeer, Wally Murphy, penned these lines in the late 1960s. The Tholsel had always been, and continues to be, the focal point in the centre of the town. The 'labour' referred to was the Department of Social Welfare Offices, which were then in the old Mechanics Institute in William Street. So, having signed on, the men came down St. Peter's Hill, and gathered to talk at the Tholsel.

The Tholsel was built in 1770, replacing the old medieval tholsel. For over one hundred years, the town corporation, assizes, petty sessions, and county courts, were held here. The corporation and the courts departed the Tholsel in December of 1890, the building was then rented out to the Hibernian Bank and is now occupied by the Bank of Ireland.

During the Civil War, the faces of the clock were shot out by Black and Tans, still based at Gormanston, and the clock was out of action for many months. The people of the town traditionally checked their watch by the Tholsel and when, in the mid-1980s, due to vandalism, the clock was not working, the local papers carried many complaints from townspeople who still relied on the Tholsel for their time-check. At that time, a letter in the Drogheda Independent from historian James Garry, had the effect of seeing the clock repaired in double-quick time.

The Tholsel

"Some hundred men with their officers, took position of Saint Peter's Church steeple, while others entered the towers of West Gate and more occupied the round tower hard by the gate called Saint Sundays. All those in the steeple of Saint Peter's were summoned by Cromwell to yield to mercy, but having noted what mercy this murder has dealt out to others they declined to come down.

Upon this he ordered his soldiers to set fire to the steeple and roasted many of them alive; and from the midst of the dreadful flames was one voice heard crying out in agony 'God damn me, God confound me, I burn, I burn', which from the methods used of calling on his maker, I would interpret that this would have been an English cavalier."

This extract comes from the writings of Randal McDonell, in a work of fiction deemed to be based on the historical facts of the Cromwellian siege of Drogheda in 1649. St. Peter's church in Peter Street was at that time said to have the highest steeple in Europe, and indeed it must have been a very large church, as it had seven chapels of ease, Saint Martin's, Saint Patrick's, Saint Peter's, Saint John's, Saint George's and Saint Anne's.

In the north east corner of the graveyard adjoining the church there is a fine medieval cadaver tombstone. It has been dated to 1520 and it covered the grave of Sir Edmond Golding and his wife Elizabeth Flemying.

The present church was erected in 1753, but the spire and porch were only put in place forty years later, to the design of Francis Johnson who live in Drogheda in the 1790s.

Saint Peter's Church of Ireland

Fairs were held in Drogheda on a monthly basis, but by far the best was the horse fair on the 12th of May. At the May fair, a farmer could buy a good plough horse or cart horse. Horses were sold to pull bread carts, milk floats, and brewer's drays, and all were on show at the fair. In addition to the horses, droves of donkeys from County Clare and County Mayo were also shown and bought by the farmers and farm labourers of Louth, Meath and Monaghan.

The May Fair was best known for the quality of horses. These were the half breeds, sired by a blood stallion out of an Irish draught mare. A foal resulting from such a cross might be anything, a racehorse, hunter or charger. They were bred by the local farmers, and were in a sense a gamble, because a good quality hunter might literally bring fame and fortune to its breeder.

Women in brown wrap-around woollen shawls would be seen selling foodstuffs from round wicker baskets. Fresh fish from Clogherhead, and sugar candy made locally, would be on sale. The horses were allowed to wander freely and could be seen grazing on the riverbank. Bassetts directory, for County Louth, records that upwards of twelve thousand horses were kept in the County in the 1880s.

Ballad singers and travelling fiddle players were a common sight at the fairs. A good ballad singer might travel considerable distances from fair to fair and make a living by his skill. His listeners were interested in his music, but they were even more interested in his song, and the best ballads were either humorous, satirical or political. Gambling was also popular, and the three-card trick-man was a familiar sight at the fair. The thimble rigger, a similar gamble using three thimbles and a pea, was also popular. Medicine men, travelled to all the fairs selling miracle cure-alls, which never worked, but they added colour to the fair. Strongmen also often appeared at the fair. Lifting cartwheels was one of their popular feats.

The Court-house, Fair Street

Writing in the Irish Times in 1977, Quidnunc i.e. Seamus O'Kelly, noted;

"In the decade coming up to 1939 the young sporting gentleman on the Army Air Corps, who happened to be training at Gormanston camp had a tendency to 'shoot the Viaduct' in their flying machines, which were of such vintage models as Gloucester Gladiators, and Avro Cadets. Indeed it is rumoured that some of the more daring bloods used to 'loop the Viaduct'".

Nowadays of course, things are much quieter, and the only thing that loops the Viaduct is the occasional swallow, full of the joys of summer. However, Sir John McNeill's great Victorian engineering feat stands as fine today as when it was first constructed in the 1850s, built to link the Belfast to Dublin railway line. Prior to this, the traveller had to disembark and travel by horse-drawn carriage across the river. McNeill was a native of Mount Pleasant, Dundalk, and was the first professor of civil engineering at Trinity College.

One of the most popular stories in Drogheda folklore is that the bridge was built on cotton wool. Jim Garry explains, writing in the journal of the Old Drogheda Society, the cofferdams were built in the river for piers 13 and 14, and in the case of any cofferdam, there will always be some seepage of water. To counteract this, the contractors used bales of wool inside the cofferdams, and when the foundations were laid, the wool was left there. Hence the mistaken belief, that the bridge was built on wool. A cofferdam is a temporary wall of concrete steel, clay or wood, built around the site for foundations of a bridge, which would be underwater or in danger of flooding, the purpose of which, is to provide an enclosed area for which water can kept out.

The bridge has twelve arches, and measures 17,000 feet. The limestone piers are 98 feet above the water. It cost £70,000 to build, the price of a small semi-detached house in today's terms.

The Viaduct

The banner painter, William Reynolds, was born at Dowth, County Meath on the 22nd September 1842. Writing about him in Ríocht na Mídhe, James Garry refers to him as "A Forgotten Meath Artist". In his short life Reynolds made his mark as one of the finest banner painters of his time in Ireland.

He was educated at Dowth where one of his classmates would have been John Boyle O'Reilly, the noted Fenian. Reynolds was also noted for his nationalist beliefs, just like O'Reilly. His gravestone bears the following inscription, scripted by Professor George Petrie:

"Pray for the soul of William Reynolds, Oldbridge, to whose memory this cross has been raised, by his friends at home and abroad, who admired him for his many virtues, sterling patriotism, and great and varied gifts and as an artist, who successfully illustrated the religious and national glories of his native land. Born 22nd September, 1842, died 13th December, 1881."

During his short lifetime, Reynolds painted somewhere in the region of sixty banners for the trades and organisations of Drogheda. He also painted a set of smaller banners for the Holy Family Confraternity in Saint Peter's Church. On all parade days in Drogheda the banners would be carried proudly by their respective societies.

Sadly, the majority of the banners no longer exist, however four of the large banners and a number of the confraternity banners are kept safely at the Millmount Museum. In 1998, the museum started a restoration programme for the banners to bring them back to their former glory and to help ensure James Garry's desire that William Reynolds will no longer be, 'A Forgotten Meath Artist'.

Millmount
Museum

On Saint Patrick's Day, 1881, the foundation stone of the new Catholic church of Saint Mary's, Drogheda, was laid by Mr Thomas Matthews. This act was blessed by Dr Nulty, the Bishop of Meath. Three years and one month later Dr Nulty returned to Drogheda to dedicate the new church. A Pontifical High Mass was celebrated by Dr. Donnelly, the Bishop of Clogher.

The new church replaced an earlier one on the site, and prior to that, on the samesite, stood the town jail. In the aftermath of the failed Spanish Armada of 1588, a group of Spanish sailors were held prisoner in Drogheda, very possibly in the jail at James's Street. The list of prisoners included drummers, ships boys, servants, clerks, and even a barber. Three of the prisoners died in jail, Don Diego de Luzon, Don Sebastian Zapata, and Antonion de Bacia. Some of the more important prisoners included Balthasar Lopez del Arbal, Sergeant Major of Naples, and Horatio Donai, Master of the Valenceara.

The church was to the design of Mr P. J. Dodd and the cost for its construction was in the region of £8000. Train excursions to the opening of the new church were organised by Great Northern Railways, and a poster advertising same can be seen in Millmount Museum.

In 1984, the church celebrated its centenary. The then parish priest, Fr. John C. O'Reilly, organised many celebrations in the church. Indeed, throughout his career as parish priest of Saint Mary's, (from 1981 until his death in May of 1998) Fr. O'Reilly made a major contribution to the development of the church. The Blessed Sacrament Chapel, the car park at the Old Hill, and the re-development of Saint Mary's graveyard, Calvary, will stand as monuments to his endeavours. He was a proud Meath man who endeared himself to many in Drogheda.

Saint Mary's, James' Street

In 1900, Thomas and Anne Reid purchased for themselves a new home and business premises at No.19, Peter Street/No.1, Fair Street, Drogheda. They were both natives of the area and in purchasing these premises they were coming home. Anne was born at nearby Magdalene Street, where her father had kept a grocery and public house. He was a noted nationalist and member of the towns corporation. Thomas was born at Ballymakenny about two miles outside the town.

Peter Street was obviously a popular place on Saturday nights, one newspaper reported with the headline:

"War in Peter Street......On Saturday night nine fights took place in Peter Street......the Kanes, Stewards, Duffies, and several other belligerent tribes were engaged in the conflicts."

One resident of the area, Judith Silverman, a daughter of a Jewish trader who lived on the corner of Magdalene Street and Fair Street writing almost forty years later recalled how much she looked forward to Saturday night to see the shenanigans outside Mr Reid's public house.

The Reid family were blessed with three children, Nano, James and Jenny, of which Nano was to achieve fame as one of the foremost Irish painters of this century. Nano first registered as a student of the Metropolitan School of Art, in Kildare Street, Dublin, in 1921. She later studied in both Paris and London, but it is sad that she only achieved true artistic freedom when she returned to Drogheda and the mystical Boyne Valley.

Nano died in her native Drogheda in 1979, leaving a legacy of wonderful artwork in many collections both private and public throughout the country. The pub her father purchased in 1900 is still preserved with a fine wooden interior looking as good as it did when the Reids purchased it 98 years ago.

Clarkes,
Peter Street

In 1881, Colr. P. Greene proposed that Mr. Charles Stuart Parnell MP should be made a Freeman of the Borough of Drogheda. This proposal was passed by the Corporation with only one dissenting voice, that of Colr. Robert B. Daly, a local auctioneer. Parnell, however, did not come to Drogheda to accept this honour until May of 1884, for in that year Colr. Casey Connelly, a noted Parnellite, was elected Mayor. Charles Stuart Parnell obviously felt it appropriate to come to Drogheda when one of his supporters was Mayor. A public holiday was declared in the town, and upwards of 20,000 people came out to view the spectacle.

At eleven o'clock in the morning Parnell arrived on board a train from Dublin. At the many train stops on his journey, people garlanded the train with flowers and by the time it reached Drogheda there were six brass bands on board ready to participate in the town's festivities. A large parade had already gathered at the railway station. All the town trade banners were carried and on display. The parade moved off with Parnell in front along with the Mayor in an open horse-drawn carriage. This was followed by more open carriages with the members of both Drogheda Corporation and Dublin Corporation in their full regalia.

Parnell addressed the gathering from the great Doric Venetian window on the side of the Mayoralty House. He was presented with the freedom scroll in a silver box with the inscription "Donated by the Nationalists of Drogheda". No-one could deny, he was indeed the uncrowned King of Ireland.

The Mayoralty House was built in 1765 to the design of Mr Hugh Darley, a Drogheda architect. It was one of the town's most important public buildings and is preserved today in excellent condition as a modern music emporium. A fine example of how an old building can be preserved and put to modern usage.

Mayoralty House (Sound Shop)

This very fine 18th Century house was built by Alderman James Barlow in 1734. It has a façade of five bays and three storeys over a vaulted basement. It has a tall pedimented Gibbsian doorcase, a fine example of this technique. The central window on the first floor is accentuated by a bracketed segmental pediment and highly decorated volutes, splayed from the top of the jambs. The interior includes a magnificent staircase with fluted balusters and Corinthian columns on the corners. The house is illustrated on Ravells' Map of Drogheda, 1749, and Gabrieli Ricciardelli's painting of 1782, which hangs in the town library.

To generations of Drogheda people the Barlow house has been identified as the local police station. The Royal Irish Constabulary moved there in 1861 and there they remained until their disbandment in 1922. In September of that year, the Garda Síochána arrived in Drogheda, and the Barlow House became their home, until they went to their new premises in the grounds of the Old Abbey in 1997.

There had always been two police barracks in Drogheda, one on the South Quay and the other in the Barlow House at West Gate. The South Quay premises were closed in 1931 and Barlow House became the main Garda station. The house has witnessed 135 years of policing in Drogheda. Countless numbers of young police and Garda recruits have passed through its doorway in that time. It would be impossible to name them all but in recalling two, Richard Darcy, a native, and Willie Green, one who made Drogheda his home, taken from us prematurely but remembered with fondness, we remember them all.

The Barlow House

The notorious Leinster highwayman, Michael Collier, was born on the hill of Bellewstown in the year 1780. Throughout a colourful career he robbed mail coaches and relieved many travellers on the road of their money and valuables. Yet the highwayman always provided a fascination for the Irish and was regarded with a certain amount of admiration.

Collier has always been portrayed as a Robin Hood-like character, robbing from the rich and helping the poor. On one occasion it is told, he visited a small farmer's cottage seeking food. The farmer's wife told Collier that her husband had been ill from typhus fever and they were forced to sell their cow to pay the rent on their farm to the local landlord, so they had no milk to give him as they had none for themselves. She advised him also that the landlord was, that day, in the adjoining townland collecting rent.

That evening as the landlord returned to his mansion he was ambushed by Collier and relieved of all his money collected in rent from his tenants. Collier returned to the farmer's house and presented them with £13, the price of their rent, and a further £10 to buy a new cow. This is the popular presentation of the benevolent highwayman. On the other hand, it has been proven that Collier was a government informer and was paid 'the black money', the term used to refer to informants' wages in Victorian times.

One of his most popular haunts was an inn on the Hungry Hall Road, which in those times was the main Drogheda – Mullingar highway. Nowadays the Hungry Hall Road is known as the Donore Road, and the only inn that exists there is the Thatch. If you enter nowadays you won't find Collier sitting at a table there, but Séamus will still give good advice on horses which might have been of interest to Collier over a century ago.

On the 13th of August, 1849, Collier entered the house of Mr Edward Reilly of West Street, Drogheda. There he died and was buried at midnight in an unmarked grave in the Cord Cemetery.

The Thatch

Margaret Bermingham was born in Skyrne, Co. Meath, in the early 1500s. In 1530 she married Bartholomew Ball, a wealthy Dublin merchant, who later was appointed Lord Mayor of Dublin. Two of their sons were also mayors of Dublin. This was Ireland of the Reformation and Walter Ball, a son of Margaret and Bartholomew, abandoned the 'old faith' and set about promoting the 'new religion'.

Margaret however adhered to the old faith supporting priests and running a private school to teach the faith to all who wished to learn it. She was warned on many occasions about her work and told to desist, but she would not. In 1581 her son Walter became Lord Mayor of Dublin. He ordered that his mother be arrested and imprisoned. Following three years of suffering, she died in prison. In September of 1992 in a ceremony in Saint Peter's Square, Rome, Margaret Ball along with 16 other martyrs, was beatified by Pope John Paul II.

The memories of the Ball family are much happier ones in Drogheda. A branch of the family first arrived here in the 14th century and their name has become synonymous with the town's history ever since. In 1412, Henry Ball received the town's Unification Charter from the King and in 1800 another member of the Ball family, acting as MP for Drogheda, argued against the Act of Union on behalf of the townspeople who were not in favour of it. Although his protestations were not successful and the Act of Union was passed, a local subscription was raised to acknowledge his endeavours on behalf of the townspeople. The fine Ball Gate, which stands beside the Bridge of Peace was purchased by the townspeople, inscribed with the coat of arms of the Ball family and erected at the entrance of Ball Estates in 1801.

In the 1950s the lands of Ballsgrove were purchased by the local authority and now incorporate the housing estates of Highfield, Ballsgrove, Saint Finian's Park and Rathmullen Park.

Ballsgrove Gate

On a dark October evening in early winter of 1940, Horst Felber and his colleague, Walter Hoppman boarded their aeroplane to do another scheduled bombing run over London. They departed from occupied France at approximately 8.00pm. Somehow during their long night, they were blown off course and found themselves flying over the Irish Sea. They crashed, or were possibly shot down, and while they both were wearing air-filled life-saving jackets, they could not have survived for long in one of the roughest, coldest seas in the world. They both were drowned never to see Germany again.

The body of Horst Felber was washed up on the shore at Mosney on the 26th October. A few days later Walker Hoppman was found on the strand at Clogherhead. Felber was buried in Mornington and Hoppman was buried at the Board of Health graveyard in Drogheda. The German Minister to Ireland attended both funerals and wreaths with red sashes bearing the swastika were laid on both graves. In 1960 both bodies were lifted and re-interred at the German graveyard in Glencree, County Wicklow.

Traditionally, a settlement for seamen, sitting at the mouth of the River Boyne. A large battlemented tower and a narrow finger-shaped tower align the mouth of the river here. They are navigational aids built in the reign of Elizabeth I, hence given the name "*The Maiden Tower and Finger*" from the maiden queen. Mornington or Marinerstown is first mentioned in a grant of Walter de Lacy to:

"The town of Mariners in Ireland near the port of Drogheda to God and the Abbey of St. Mary in Furness in England and the abbot and monks serving there".

Mornington

At the turn of the century in Laytown, Mr. Carroll could offer the discerning customer water baths to which salt water was pumped from the sea. In nearby Bettystown Thomas Simcocks provided *'sea bathing in pure salt water, hot or cold.'* The nearby Alverno Hotel was described in glowing terms by a writer for the Drogheda Independent in 1885:

> *"Taking it all in all, he says, I cannot convey to you my admiration and esteem for it. At the outset it is notable, that not one visitor here, and they are many and of the most respectable class, has left it for the last five weeks; that the invalids have become convalescent and the strong still stronger; that they all, Catholic and Protestant, live and mix together on terms of the most social unity vying all of them to make each other happy and cheerful".*

What a wonderful place it must have been! What a wonderful world when a reporter for the Drogheda Independent could spend five weeks in a hotel barely ten miles from the newspaper office.

The highlight of the year at Laytown will always be the annual strand races. After all, Laytown has the only race track in the world that is watered twice a day, three hundred and sixty five days a year. The railway offered special return fares for the races from Dublin in 1846, at the rate of four shillings for first class, three shillings for second class, and two shillings for third class. The races were traditionally held in August but in recent years have been held in June.

The village of Julianstown is divided in four by the main Belfast-Dublin road running north-south and the river Nanny flowing west-east to enter the sea at Laytown. Indeed the first references to the area refer to it as the Parish of Aney, a derivative of Ainge, a Gaelic word for Nanny.

It cannot be ascertained where the name 'Julian' emerged from, but one poet informs us thus;

"A lovely lady gave thee thy name
A lady of much charm and fame
A lady a-whom did ride to hounds
Across the richest of Royal Meath grounds."

The lady referred to is Juliana Preston, the wife of Lord Gormanstown, whose estates bordered Julianstown.

The area is steeped in a rich folklore, for it is said that at nearby Mosney Wood, St. Patrick baptised his first convert, Benignus. It is also said that St. Patrick cursed the Nanny River and as a result no salmon can be found there.

In 1641, the Old Irish of Ulster rose in armed rebellion against the King. Sir Henry Tichbourne, Governor of Drogheda, appealed to Dublin for help against the rebellious Old Irish. A force of six hundred foot and fifty horsemen were despatched from Dublin to relieve Drogheda, which was now besieged. The rebels decided to ambush the relief column arriving from Dublin. A Colonel Plunkett was charged by Rory O'Moore to lead the operation. The relief force was ambushed and practically wiped out by Plunkett's troops at Julianstown Bridge in November of 1641.

In the Church of Ireland graveyard lie the mortal remains of Jane Tandy, wife of the Irish patriot James Napper Tandy, immortalised in the ballad *"The Wearing of the Green".* Tandy had many business connections with the Drogheda area indeed, he was a freeman of the borough of Drogheda. However, he was struck off the freedom list when he arrived with the French at Killala in 1798. The minute book of the Drogheda Corporation's records reads:

"Disenfranchised having landed off the coast of Ireland with the enemy."

Julianstown

In 1690, James II gave John Bellew the title Lord Duleek. Although Bellew was an important Jacobite supporter he took no part in the Battle of the Boyne (1690). The following year he was wounded at the Battle of Aughrim, where upwards on 11,000 Jacobites were killed. It is said the Irish ran away at Aughrim. John Bellew's headstone in Duleek graveyard highlights his wound perhaps suggesting he was not running away.

"This tomb hath being repaired and the vault made by Dame Mary Bermingham of Dunfort wife to John Lord Bellew who was shot in the belly in Oughrim fight the first of July 1691".

Bellew took his title from the village of Duleek which is on the banks of the River Nanny in Co. Meath. The village is believed to have been the site of the ancient Christian settlement of "Damhliag Chianain" meaning the stone house of Cianan. When St. Patrick first arrived in Ireland, there were already a number of the native Irish converted to Christanity. Cianan was one of these and so Patrick appointed him a Bishop.

In 1171 our old friends, The Four Masters note:

"Duleek this year was plundered by the Knights of Milo de Cogan and some of them were slain on the following day by the Danes of Dublin".

So, barely one year after their arrival in Ireland, the Normans were active in the Duleek area. The Normans asserted their control by building castles in the areas they conquered. Duleek was no different, and while there is no trace of it now, the Normans did build a castle there.

In 1821 George IV visited the Conyngham family at nearby Slane and during his time there, paid a visit to Annsbrook House in Duleek. In anticipation of this visit, Mr Smith, the owner, had a large dining room added to the main building. In the "Houses of Ireland" de Breffny notes;

"When the diarrhoetic King finally arrived, the August sun shone brightly and whether from a sudden whim or a feeling of claustrophobia at entering Annsbrook with all his retinue, he requested to dine al fresco, and thus he never saw the new dining room".

Duleek

The Williamite ballad "Lilliburlero" refers to Lord Tyrconnell ie Richard Talbot as a jackass. Richard Talbot was no mean warrior; he had served in the royalist garrison that had defended Drogheda against Oliver Cromwell in September of 1649.

Richard Talbot escaped the siege and subsequent slaughter of the garrison, and went to live at the court of the King of Spain. There he remained until the end of Cromwellian Protectorate and the restoration of the Stewart monarchy, in the guise of Charles II to the throne of England. For his seemingly miraculous escape from Drogheda, he earned the nickname "Fighting Dick Talbot". Cromwell himself writing to Lentel, the speaker of the House of Commons, said, "*Today at Drogheda I put three thousand to the sword*".

On the 1st of July 1690 "Fighting Dick" sat on the hill of Donore with 5,000 men facing an advancing army of 27,000 Williamites. Meanwhile King James II, with the bulk of the Jacobite forces, was off to the west at Rossnaree, too far away to be able to help Talbot. It is no surprise therefore, that Donore Hill was taken and the remaining Jacobites routed barely four hours after the battle had begun. As the armies of William marched down the hill into the Boyne, their pipes and drums played "Lilliburlero". Facing such monumental odds, one can't help but wonder, did Talbot feel like the jackass, he was likened to in the tune.

Donore

The People of Drogheda

The arrival of the Anglo-Normans in Ireland in the 1170s, was forever to change the landscape of the country. The area they first dominated was known as the Pale, and all along its perimeters from Drogheda to Wexford, Norman castles began to appear. The area surrounding Drogheda and the Boyne Valley was no different.

The Kingdom of Meath, containing modern Meath, Westmeath and parts of Offaly, was granted to Hugh de Lacy in 1172. Immediately de Lacy began to secure his new lands by building castles around its perimeters. The site of Drogheda, on the banks of the navigable River Boyne, provided the perfect location for the establishment of a new town. A wooden fortress was built on the mound now known as Millmount, a typical Norman Motte and Bailey.

On the river banks below it, a town began to develop, which was to become known as Novus Pons, or Drocda, and finally Drogheda, an Anglicisation of the Irish Droichead Atha. The name, Bridge of the Ford, it is now generally accepted, comes from the site known in modern times as Oldbridge. This was the main crossing point of the Boyne in the early Medieval period and the Normans took this name for their new town of Drogheda. The current site of the town is not fordable at the river, however it is the narrowest point across which a bridge could be built. So, effectively, the Oldbridge site was no longer used and the new bridge site at Drogheda was now the main crossing point on the Boyne.

Hugh de Lacy continued into the 1180s with his building and development plans until, in 1186 at Durrow, he decided to knock down a monastery and use its raw materials, stone, etc. to build a castle. One local did not take this proposal very well and entered de Lacy's camp and proceeded to decapitate him with an axe leaving the Kingdom of Meath with no Overlord. De Lacy's eldest son, Walter, had not reached his maturity and so was ineligible to claim his father's titles.

In 1189, Richard I (the Lionheart) succeeded his father, Henry II, as King of England. The following year he led the Third Crusade to the Holy Land to save Jerusalem. He left his brother, Prince John or John Lackland, in charge of affairs in England while he was away on crusade. The young de Lacy now began to petition for his father's lands. John however, saw an opportunity to gain some land for himself as his surname suggests he did not have any.

The first major battle of the Second Crusade was at the city of Acre. When the crusaders took control of the city, Richard I claimed all the goods and profits from the city for himself. This decision was not welcomed by the Austrians who immediately withdrew and returned home. The crusade continued until 1192 when Richard and the great leader of the Muslims, Saladin, having effectively beaten each other to a standstill, agreed a truce and a treaty was drawn up. Richard now decided to return to England but on the return journey his ship sank and he was forced to travel over land. While travelling through Austria he was kidnapped by the Austrians, who obviously hadn't forgiven him for his actions in the aftermath of the siege of Acre, and held for ransom. When the ransom was eventually paid, Richard returned to England where Walter de Lacy, now having reached his maturity, successfully petitioned the king for his father's titles and lands, and was granted them in May 1194.

To assert his new found power, Walter granted a charter to the town of Drogheda, confirming to all his tenants the rights of the law of Breuteil. These laws were a recognised set of town laws in the medieval period. Breuteil was a small town on the river Vico in Northern Normandy. The laws entitled the colonists a certain size of land plot, grazing land for their cattle and fishing rights along the Boyne as far as Trim. It is said de Lacy inhabited the town with the men of the Welsh Marches. The native Irish did not welcome the new visitors to the area and there are many references to attacks by them on the new settlers. The new settlers in turn complained to their Norman overlords that they wanted protection from these attacks. In 1234 a murage charter was granted to Drogheda (le mur being French for wall). This murage charter gave the municipal authority the right to levy a tax on all goods being imported through the town's port to pay for the building of town walls. The town walls and gates enclosed an area of 113 acres making Drogheda and Kilkenny, the biggest walled towns in Ireland, being approximately half the size of the walled city of London and twice the size of the walled city of Dublin.

In the early years of the town development, two towns began to develop, one on each side of the riverbank. One became known as Drogheda in Meath, and the other as Drogheda in Oriel. This situation continued until 1412 when a unification charter was granted and the two towns became one.

From its first development, Drogheda became an important port town with goods being imported from and exported to many parts of the world. To Ayr, Carlisle, Chester, Cardiff, Southampton and London on the English coast and to further afield Iceland, Gdansk, Calais, Dieppe and Bordeaux, and as far south as Lisbon in Portugal. It also became an important ecclesiastical centre with the arrival of all the major mendicant orders in the 13th Century. The Synod of Kells in 1140 decreed that the Boyne would be the natural border between the archdiocese of Armagh and the diocese of Meath. With the towns establishing on either side of the riverbank there was one in each diocese. Even after unification, this situation remained and does to the present day, with the south side in St. Mary's parish in the Diocese of Meath, and the north side in St. Peter's parish in the archdiocese of Armagh.

In the mid-1340s the bubonic plague or 'Black Death' as it came to be known swept Europe arriving in Ireland in 1348. A Franciscan friar, John Clyn, recorded in his journals:

"…in the months of September and October, bishops, prelates, priests, friars, noblemen and others, women as well as men, came in great numbers from every part of Ireland to the pilgrimage centre That Molyngis (Teach Molinge on the River Barrow). So great were their numbers that on many days it was possible to see thousands of people flocking there; some true devotion but others (the majority indeed) through fear of the plague, which then was very prevalent. It began near Dublin, at Howth, and at Drogheda. These cities were almost entirely destroyed and emptied of inhabitants so that in Dublin alone, between the beginning of August and Christmas, 14,000 people died."

Friar John Clyn also noted that, of his own order, the Friars Minor (Franciscans), twenty-five died in their house at Drogheda of the plague. It has been suggested that Clyn's figures are inflated, however it should be noted that Richard Fitzralph, the Archbishop of Armagh, visited the town in 1349 to preach to the townspeople because of the ravages of the plague.

The town was steadily developing trade links as is illustrated by the enterprise of Nicholas Abbot of Drogheda, Richard Byrne of Dublin, Jenkin Alderseye, John Glover of Chester, John Symkoke and Robert Preston of Drogheda. In February 1457 they freighted a Drogheda ship to sail to Westmony in Iceland with Irish goods 'well suited' as they said, to trade in Iceland. It was their intention to trade their goods for fish which in turn could be sold on the Irish markets. When the ship arrived in Iceland, the season for fish was past and all the fish had already been taken by English merchants. Abbot, Byrne, Alderseye and Glover were there in person, but Symkoke and Preston had sent representatives. They all consulted and Abbot agreed to stay over in Iceland to sell their goods and have ready a return cargo for the next season, and the others agreed to send a ship the following May. Unfortunately they did not and eighteen months later when Abbot managed to get a ship home he sued them in parliament for his losses of forty-five pounds. However, he ran into the usual problems of overseas traders; contracts made abroad were not admissible in common law courts.

The dissolution in 1539 saw the closing of all of Drogheda's monasteries and hospitals run by religious orders, with their lands and properties in general handed over to the town's Corporation. An act of Elizabeth in 1560 saw Drogheda lose its parliamentary status meaning that parliaments from now on could only be held at Dublin.

Records show that parliament had sat in Drogheda on eighteen occasions in the High Medieval period. The most famous one being that of December 1494 which passed the noted Poyning's Law. This law stipulated that never again could the King's authority be employed legislatively in Ireland without sanction from England. The members of Grattan's Parliament were still campaigning in the 1780s to have Poyning's Law repealed.

Throughout the 1500s and into the 1600s the Catholic faith remained strong in Drogheda. Fr. Henry Fitzsimons, a Jesuit, relates in 1606 how almost the entire population of Drogheda was prevailed upon to go to Protestant churches for fear of being imprisoned. Catholics captured in the streets of Drogheda were brought before the Lord Deputy and questioned on their religion. One local man, by the name of Barnwell, on being asked to accompany the Lord Deputy to church in 1607, went with Chichester as far as the door of the church before saying;

"This far, sir, God and my conscience allow me to accompany you, but no farther."

The man was struck on the head and dragged into the church where he lay unconscious and died shortly after.

In 1641, the old English and Catholic communities rose up against their new English overlords. The first meeting of these 'Confederates' as they came to be known was held on the hill on Knockcrofty in Co. Meath, in modern times known as Crufty, about three miles south of Drogheda. The town of Drogheda was besieged for nine months although this would not be its most famous siege of the 1640s.

In September of 1649 the town, now in the hands of a Royalist Garrison under Sir Henry Aston, was besieged by Oliver Cromwell, the Lord Protector. The Cromwellian forces spent a week preparing for the attack on the town. At eight o'clock on the morning of September 19th, Aston was summoned to surrender;

Sir,

> *Having brought the army belonging to the parliament of England before this place, to reduce it to obedience, to the end the effusion of blood may be prevented, I thought it fit to summon you to deliver the same into my hands to their use. If this be rejected you will have no cause to blame me.*

> *I expect your answer and rest,*
> *Your servant,*
> *O. Cromwell*

Aston refused and so the bombardment of the town began. The siege lasted for two days. When it was broken, Cromwell ordered that all who were in arms were to be put to the sword. He further commanded that the officers and every tenth man of the rank and file were to be killed, and the rest were shipped as slaves to Barbados. Every priest found in the town was executed. Lieutenant Colonel Boyle was at dinner in Drogheda five days after the initial massacre, with Lady Moore, sister to the Earl of Sutherland, when one of Cromwell's soldiers is reputed to have entered and whispered in his ear that he was to be put to death. As he rose from the table, Lady Moore asked where he was going. His answer was simple, *"Madame, to die"*. He was shot immediately on stepping out of the room.

Thomas A. Wood, a parliamentarian soldier since 1643, was obviously shocked by what he saw in Drogheda. His brother recorded his testimony:

"It was the winter after the siege. At which time, being often with his mother and brethren, he (Thomas) would tell them of the most terrible assaulting and storming of Drogheda. Wherein he himself had been engaged … He told them that when they were to make their way up to the lofts and galleries in the church and up to the tower where the enemy had fled, each of the assailants would take up a child and use it as a buckler of defence when they ascended the steps, to keep themselves from being shot or brained. After they had killed all in the church they went into the vaults underneath, where all the flower, and choicest of the women and ladies had hid themselves. One of these, a most handsome virgin, and arrayed in costly and gorgeous clothes, kneeled down to Thomas Wood with tears and prayers to save her life; and being struck with profound pity, took her under his arm, went with her out of the church, with intentions to put her over the works and let her shift for herself; but then a soldier, perceiving his intentions, ran a sword up her belly, whereupon Mr. Wood, seeing her gasping, took away her money, jewels, etc., and flung her down over the works."

Cromwell himself reported that only 64 men under his command had been killed, and 100 wounded. 29 enemy cavalry officers, 48 infantry officers, 220 reformadoes and troopers and *"2,500 foot soldiers beside staff officers, surgeons etc. and many inhabitants"* were killed. Of course modern day revisionist historians tell us none of this happened but the debate is not yet resolved and revisionism by its very nature must be open to revision.

In 1690, the sound of cannon fire was to be heard once again in the Drogheda area. On the 1st July, King William and King James, with their respective armies confronted each other at what King James described as *"an indifferent good post"* James had ordered Lord Iveagh, with his foot regiment, and some other reinforcements numbering 1,300 men, to hold the walled town of Drogheda. The battle took place about two miles west of Drogheda and with the retreat of King James, William was victorious. On the 2nd July, Brigadier de la Mellonier with 1,000 horse and 300 foot plus eight field guns arrived outside Drogheda demanding its surrender. James had placed Brian Magennis, the Fifth Viscount Iveagh, in charge but he had fled westward leaving Brigadier William Tuite in charge. Tuite was put under pressure by an anxious townspeople who did not want a repeat of the events of 1649 and he decided to surrender. The Jacobite officers were allowed to keep their swords but all other arms had to be laid down. On the 3rd July, the garrison marched out of Drogheda towards Athlone. An English regiment now occupied the town and George Storey recorded: *"The English officers took great care to preserve the town from the violence of the soldiers"*. Drogheda, in view of its past treatment at the hands of the English, was to be treated with kid gloves so that the Irish would not feel their situation to be hopeless.

Throughout the 1700s, Catholics were still by far the majority of the population of the town with many wealthy Catholic merchants living there. Defenderism was rampant and it is no surprise that in 1792 three local Catholic merchants were brought before the courts for seditious activities. Their legal team, comprised of the eminent barrister John Phillpot Curran, and a young junior counsel,

Theobald Wolfe Tone, a barrister endeavouring to make a name for himself on the Leinster Circuit. As a result of this case, Tone became the agent of the Catholic committees, continuing on his journey to becoming a founder of the United Irishmen. In his journals, Tone described having a pleasant evening in Drogheda at the home of James Bird, the chairman of the Catholic committee, in the company of *'a parcel of girls'* but he described the town as being *'a collection of mudwall cabins surrounded by ancient walls'*. Another noted United Irishman in Drogheda at this time was James Napper Tandy, immortalised in the ballad 'The Wearing of the Green'. He purchased for himself the freedom of Drogheda in 1790, for business reasons as he had substantial business interests in the town, and to give him the right to vote in the town. In 1798, Tandy arrived at Killala with the French. The Drogheda Corporation immediately struck

him off the list of freemen. The minutes record *"disenfranchised, having landed off the coast with the enemy"*.

In 1862, Thomas Clarke Luby inaugurated a branch of the Fenian movement in Drogheda, when six of its citizens took the Fenian Oath. Patrick Leonard, a native of Tullyallen was in charge of the Drogheda Fenians. He had gained his military experience fighting in the Civil War on the union side in America. A countrywide insurrection was planned for March 1867, and the Drogheda members made their move on Shrove Tuesday, 5th March. Through the night, groups of men began to gather at various points throughout the town. The papers reported upwards of 1,000 men gathered, however this was a gross exaggeration. Hughes' History of Drogheda, 1893, records that only 150 men actually participated. In its aftermath about 25 local men were arrested. Only four of them were charged, and eventually sentenced to transportation to Western Australia. They were Patrick Wall, Robert May, and Luke and Laurence Fullham. The Fullhams died in Australia but Robert May and Patrick Wall eventually returned to Drogheda. Wall however then went to America. Among their fellow prisoners on board the prison ship the 'Houghomont' was John Boyle O'Reilly, one of the most famous Fenians and a native of Dowth, about four miles west of Drogheda.

In the aftermath of the death of Charles Stewart Parnell, the Drogheda Corporation remained loyal to the old Nation Party, and in 1906 John Redmond was made a freeman of the town. In 1912, it seemed at last that Home Rule was to become a reality. In Ulster, Carson formed the Ulster Volunteer Force to resist Home Rule and defend Ulster against the break with the Union. Eoin McNeill, writing in

Pearse's publication *'An Claidheamh Solais', 'the Sword of Light'*, said the Unionists were right and the Nationalists should do the same. Pearse said the only thing funnier than a Unionist with a gun was a Nationalist without one. All over the country rallies were held to organise the Irish Volunteers. In Drogheda a public meeting was held on the Mall, addressed by Eoin McNeill and Tom Kettle, urging Drogheda men to join their organisation. The papers reported that a crowd of 4,000 gathered at the Mall and about 200 signed up as members of the Volunteers. The outbreak of the First World War saw Home Rule side-lined until such time as the war ended. This very issue caused a split in the volunteer movement, with the vast majority of its members, at the request of John Redmond enlisting in the British Army to go and fight for the rights of small nations. The Drogheda Advertiser on 22nd January 1916, reported that there were now over

300 local men fighting at various battle sites in and around Europe. There were also two nurses, Miss Thornhill and Miss Bessy Long of Queensborough, serving in military hospitals.

The outbreak of the 1916 Rising in Dublin was condemned by the Drogheda Corporation who demanded that the authorities bring these ruffians to heel. In Drogheda 13 local men were arrested and imprisoned for their republican sympathies. The Drogheda Independent reported;

"On Wednesday night a large number of arrests were made by the police authorities at Drogheda of suspected parties in Drogheda, Ardee and Dunleer. The Drogheda arrests, to the number of 13, were made at a late hour at night or in the early hours of Thursday morning, by a party of police and military under DI

Carbery, and all took place simultaneously. The following are reported to have been taken into custody in Drogheda:- Messrs Wm F M Quillan, Fair Street described as the proprietor of a sack factory in Dublin; John Philip Monaghan, Chord Road, science teacher; Michl Harkin, North Strand , Report, Drogheda Advertiser; J. O'Kiely, Gaelic Teacher, Chord Road,; Joseph Carr, Black Bull, Assistant Town Clerk; M. Keenan, railway clerk, Thos Burke, Duleek Street; Thos Halpin, Stockwell Lane, and Tom Gavin, Duleek Street.

P.J. McMahon, Ardee, was arrested by DI Carbery, and brought by him to Drogheda in a motor car, and Messrs – Wrenn, James Farrelly, and Thos Mathews, Ardee, were also arrested.

At Dunleer, J. Lang, schoolmaster; Thos Kelly, James Kelly, James Butterly, John

Butterly, and Michl Reynolds, described as captain of the local corps of Volunteers, were also arrested. These latter five were for some days in possession of Barmeath Tower which they defended, subsequently surrendering to the police and military."

The general election of 1918 was to bring about a seachange in Irish politics. The old National party was defeated and Sinn Féin, with its abstentionist policy, won the vast majority of the seats fought. for. The constituency of Louth/Meath, of which Drogheda was part, was a five seater and it returned five Sinn Féin candidates. The local elections of January 1920 gave Sinn Féin a majority on Drogheda Corporation for the first time. They won 13 of the 24 seats and Philip Monaghan was elected first Sinn Féin Mayor of the town. In November 1920, speaking to the House of Commons, Lloyd George declared *"In Ireland, we have murder by the throat"* but the following weekend Michael Collins replied by having 14 British agents assassinated in Dublin. In the months that followed 'tit for tat' killings and reprisal murders became the order of the day. On February 9th, 1921 Alderman Thomas Halpin and Seán Moran were taken from their houses in the early hours and murdered on the Mornington Road by 'persons unknown' according to the inquest, but the townspeople blamed the Black and Tans. In July 1921 a truce was declared which eventually led to the signing of the Anglo-Irish Treaty on 6th December 1921. While the treaty saw the departure of the British it also, sadly, paved the way for Civil War in Ireland. In Drogheda the Anti-Treaty forces, or Republicans, took control of Millmount Barracks on the departure of the British Army, on 28th January 1922. The Free State army moved into the town in large numbers during May 1922. Subsequently conflict emerged and on 4th July the Free State army used artillery, indeed the same gun that had been used to shell the Four Courts in Dublin, to remove the Republicans from Millmount. While there was some minor conflicts in the town in the months that followed, the Civil War was effectively over for Drogheda, and this was further resolved by the order to lay down arms from Frank Aiken, commander in chief of the IRA, in May 1923.

Parallel to these political developments, Drogheda also developed on the industrial front. The 17th and 18th centuries saw Drogheda develop as a main linen manufacturing area. By the mid-1800s 2,500 people were engaged in manufacturing linen in their own homes. A town linen hall was built in 1774 in Dominic Street and according to D'Alton:

'Coarse linen sail cloth, canvas ticken,
table and towel cloth, and sheeting, to the value of £10,000 used to be the average expenditure in this hall on a Saturday.'

In 1809, 4,432,575 yards of linen were produced, and in 1823, 3,526,382 yards of plain linen cloth were exported from the town. The introduction of the power loom caused much unemployment among the handweavers. By the mid-1800s four large linen mills were operating in the town, these were Oates Mill at Greenhills, St. Mary's Mill on the Marsh Road, West Gate Mills and Mell Flax Mill. At peak times these mills employed upwards of 1,500 people.

In 1835, Thomas Grendon established an iron foundry and engineering works in the town. By 1845 he was employing upwards of 1,800 people, and at the time was manufacturing locomotives, ships, weighing machines and all classes of ironwork. The town could also boast two large breweries, Casey Connelly's at Mell, where two to three hundred barrels of beer a week were brewed; and Cairnes Brewery on the Marsh Road, where five hundred barrels a week were brewed. Jameson's operated a large distillery in Stockwell Street and, while it closed down in the 1960s, its main product, Preston 10 year old whiskey, is still a much sought-after commodity by whiskey connoisseurs. Flour-milling and the production of oatmeal was carried on by Smith and Smyth Ltd. on Merchants Quay who ground 40,000 barrels of wheat and 60,000 barrels of oats annually. Also on Constitution Hill, Nathaniel Hill had established, in 1824, a mill to produce 'Miller's Pride' oatmeal. The Drogheda Chemical Manure Company was also a major employer in the town at this time, employing over 200 people. They produced for home sale and export superphosphate special manure, dis-solved bones, bone manure, bone compound, potato, grass and turnip manures.

The majority of these industries were developed along the quaysides of Drogheda providing easy access to the ships that would carry the finished products abroad. The quays area itself provided much employment with a large amount of labour intensive work loading and unloading ships, long before the advent of the hydraulic crane. Drogheda Port acted as a main centre of export for cattle and sheep from the rich grazing lands of Co.Meath. Passenger services were also provided carrying both emigrants and visitors to England by boat practically on a daily basis. In the twelve months of 1866 and 1867, the list of emigrants registered at West Gate RIC barracks, bound for America, England, and Australia is shown in the following table. In all, 5,227 people emigrated.

Month	America		England		Total
	Males	Females	Males	Females	
Aug 1886	32	28	282	83	427
Sept	37	31	215	81	366
Oct	54	49	207	78	388
Nov	45	42	178	102	367
Dec	17	19	170	70	276
Jan 1867	5	4	107	32	148
Feb	43	29	225	63	360
March	68	51	301	40	460
April	150	102	364	69	685
May	163	102	311	80	656
June	101	72	515	91	779
July	28	19	205	83	315
TOTAL	743	548	3080	852	5227

The peace that emerged in the aftermath of the Civil War, 1922, saw Drogheda go from strength to strength in its town development. The town began to spread out, creating suburbs with an extensive house building programme by the Drogheda Corporation supported by the government from the 1930s through to the 1950s. The mud-wall thatched houses of the 1800s began to disappear, to be replaced by sturdy brick and stone houses in many new areas that had once been greenfield sites. Pearse Park, Bothar Brugha, Yellowbatter, on the northside, and on the south, Halpin Terrace, Moran's Terrace and Marian Park. In the 1960s the Ball estate, having been acquired by the corporation, provided the lands for the housing estates of Ballsgrove and, in the 1970s, Rathmullen Park and St. Finian's Park. The 1960s also saw the emergence of new lighter industries, and the early development of the Donore Road industrial estate. The first three factories established here in 1964 were Classic, a German clothes manufacturer, Hauni, a conveyor belt machine manufacturer, Becton Dickinson, a medical products manufacturer and the only one that still remains of the original three. Also in the 1960s, Irish Cement, the last of the heavy industries on the quay, moved its production centre to Platin, about three miles west of Drogheda, although the plant was taken over by Premier Periclase. The arrival in Drogheda in the 1970s of manufacturers like Coca-Cola, Thorsmans, Bissell, and IFF, helped the employment situation although unemployment still remains a major problem in the town to the present day.

Modern Drogheda continues to develop: Private housing schemes and municipal housing schemes are expanding the town almost on a weekly basis. Sadly, many of its old fine buildings are gone and very little of the Medieval fabric of the town remains but there is still a great sense of history in this old town. Long may it remain.

Sources

Journal of the Old Drogheda Society No's 1-11

Journal of the Co. Louth Archaeological Society (various)

Ríocht na Midhe (various)

Drogheda Independent, 1884 onwards

Drogheda Corporation Minutes, 1798

Annals of the Four Masters

Beresford Ellis, Peter	The Boyne Water	Blackstaff, 1976
Buckley, Victor	Archaelogical Survey Co. Louth	Dublin, 1991
Burke, Ciaran	A Walk Down Memory Lane	Private, 1996
Corgan, Anthony	Diocese of Meath, Ancient and Modern	Dublin, 1867
D'Alton, John	History of Drogheda	Drogheda, 1884
Duffner, Patrick	The Low Lane Church	Augustinians, 1979
Elliot, Marianne	Wolfe Tone	Yale, 1989
Garry, James	The Streets and Lanes of Drogheda	ODS, 1997

Gwynne & Hadcock	**Medieval Religious Houses in Ireland**	Longman, 1988
Garner, William	**Drogheda Architechtural Heritage**	FF, 1986
Hughes, Anne	**History of Drogheda**	Argus, 1983
McCullen, John	**The Call of Saint Mary's**	Private, 1984
McEvoy, Michael	**Return to the Bullring**	ODS, 1998
McKenna, Patsy	**From the Boyne to the Mournes**	Private, 1994
O'Boyle, Enda	**A History of Duleek**	DHS, 1989
Robinson, Aidan	**Ancient Drogheda**	Private, 1994
Scott, Michael	**The River Gods**	Real Ireland, 1991
Trench, C.E.F	**Slane**	Private, 1976
Zaczek, Ian	**Irish Legends**	Gill and Macmillan, 1998

Dear Reader

We hope you have found this book both enjoyable and useful. This is just one of our range of illustrated titles. Other areas currently featured include:–

Strangford's Shores
Dundalk & North Louth
Armagh

The Mournes
Belfast, the City
The Donegal Highlands

Also available in our "Illustrated History & Companion Range" are:-

Ballycastle and the Heart of the Glens
Larne and the Road to the Glens
Coleraine and the Causeway Coast
Bangor
Ballymoney
Lisburn
Newtownards

Ballymena
Banbridge
City of Derry
Hillsborough
Holywood
Newry

The paintings featured in each of the above titles are also available as signed artists prints.

If you require any further information please call or fax us on (080) 1247 883876, E-Mail us on cottage_publ@online.rednet.co.uk or write to:–

Cottage Publications
15 Ballyhay Road
Donaghadee, Co. Down
N. Ireland, BT21 0NG